Reflections and Now

Reflections and Now

Ocean Shackleton

LOVE
MATTERS

Reflections and Now
Published by Love Matters Ministries

@2024 by Ocean Shackleton
Cover design by Dylann Rhea

Correspondence to:
Reverend Ocean Shackleton at Love Matters Ministries
P.O. Box 1551
Burnsville, NC
28714

Published 2024.
First edition.

ISBN: 979-8-99189450-0

Collections

EarthBound
-Poems of nature-
Night Shadows
-Poems of sorrow-
Heart Space
-Poems of light-

EarthBound

Dawning

I love to wander by the sea
where sea breezes blow constantly,
sit on the pier at start of day,
savoring sweet salty spray,
watching the sun rise from the sea.

Kaleidoscopic art for me.
The greatest daily show on Earth,
each new day giving birth.

The Voice

Listen for the voice of Spirit.
In the silence we can hear it.
Spirit's voice is ever speaking
all the answers we are seeking.

Directions for making every choice
may be found in Spirit's voice.
In application love is found,
opportunities abound.

Listen

Listen to the music
 as the wind blows through the tree.
Inhale the scent of mountains
 infused within the breeze.

Music is created by falling water's splash.
Watching a red maple leaf come slowly
spinning past.

Note the peace within your being,
mirrored in everything you're seeing.

Lean back against the giant oak,
in the shadows that are cast,
and realized it's happened.
You are free at last.

Winter's Garden

Snow is clinging to the roses,
golden flowers through white crusts.
Icey air nips ears and noses.
We shiver at each icy gust.

There's a quiet which overwhelms,
even the rustle of the leaves.
The Earth is silent in its realmes,
a silence that each snowflake weaves.

Wood is racked upon the back porch,
waiting to be a cheery fire,
drawing frost from toes and fingers,
as the flames leap ever higher.

Time for silent meditation,
to enjoy each passing day.
Silently awaiting moments
when spring and summer have their way.

When, again, the rose bush blooms,
tiny shoots break through the earth.
When seconds become gossamer,
the spring garden knows rebirth.

Sounding Spirit

Like wisps of vapor,
we are borne about,
drifting through the realms of spirit,
rustling the leaves of eternity
like morning mists
caressing flower petals.

There's a rushing wind
composed of spirit.
Listen carefully.
You'll hear it.

The sound of starlight
ruffling the surface of the sea.
The eternal sound of spirit
formed as you and me.

The sound of sunbeams
tickling the surface of our skin.

Causing us to giggle
as its energy comes in.

Spring

Spring has burst upon the scene.
Every passing hour,
foliage on each tree gets greener,
and many little flowers
from seeds buried in the earth
spring up with all their glory.

Every hidden seed gives birth,
they tell the springtime story.

Mountain Rose

Like swirls of snowflakes, petals falling.
Distant whippoorwills are calling.
Scent of roses, titillating.
Deep peace comes to all those waiting.
Dewdrops, bemist mountain grass,
tickle bare feet as they pass.
Mountain zephyrs kiss the skin,
as we watch the day begin.
Life, encased in mountain roses,
Delicacies for eyes and noses.
Springs flow into mountain brooks,
to mountain streams through quiet nooks.
Birds flitting through the trees,
each one unique, like you and me.
I've found a delightful way,
happy, joyous, and free today.

Prelude to the Owl and the Pussycat

One of my big animal encounters occurred as I was sitting
at my table reading a book.
I heard a loud thump and a cat scream at my front door.
I went to the door, opened it and there was a huge
 horned owl lying on its back looking up at me.
It had misjudged the distance to the cat he wanted for
dinner, hit my door and knocked itself out. I tell the
 story in verse.

The Owl and the Pussycat

A dusky eve, I heard a thump
and a cat a-screaming.
I opened my door, found a lump,
a huge owl, was I dreaming?
The owl thought he would have a cat
this evening for his dinner.
But, he misjudged and hit my door,
the pussycat's a winner.
He escaped those clutching claws
and sped away on kitty paws.
I gazed into that Great Owls eyes,
listened to its painful cries.
I spoke softly to its face
then watched as it took its place
soaring in the moonlit sky.
That mystic breeze drew a sigh,
from deep within my inner core.
Nature, once again, brings more

pleasure as I observe the law
reenacted without flaw.
Survival of the fittest reigns.
One lucky kitty cat remains.

Cardinal Rule

And on the railing of the porch
a cardinal so fiery he may scorch.
The railing as he struts,
his little footprints creating ruts.
And every brace of geese that fly
a powerful magnet to the eye,
that swiftly vie for our attention.
Joys too numerous to mention.

Joys II

A panorama of emerald green,
the prettiest lawn I've ever seen.
A wood border on the left,
but, the lake's edge is bereft.
Of that density of wood,
leaving a lakeview so good
that on the lake I see a swan,
fairy images beyond the lawn.
A cluster there, attached trees,
the vista drives me to my knees.
A chanticleer with blooms white,
at the lawns edge, quite a sight.
And all the creation of the hill
blooms beginning, daffodils.
Turkeys strutting on the lawn,
Accompany the first rays of dawn.

Earthbound

Living waters, bubbling voices
speaking constantly of choices,
telling us that we are Spirit.
Listen quietly and you'll hear it.

Green forest brothers all surround,
their gift to their two footed brothers,
their essence joined in whispered sound,
fragrance wafting earthbound mothers.

We have always been one spirit.
Feel Mother's pulse, sounds of drumming.
Earthen wisdom, as we near it,
draws our brethren. They are coming.

All shall gather in this space,
every creed and every race,
touching fire, air and water,
every seeking son and daughter.

Father/Mother God, we ask:
Unite us in our common task.
Fill us. Meet each human need,
and let each loving act be seed
in universal gardens growing,
multiplying from each sowing.

As each loving act is done,
their warmth be greater than the sun,
enveloping a fruitful earth,
as love's new age shall have its birth.

The River

The river of life is always flowing,
we oft don't know where it is going.
Those things we won't know till the end,
there are surprises round the bend.
Around the bend there shall be much,
some of which we'll get to touch.
As long as we are in the flow,
the river knows where it should go.
Sometimes we struggle to change direction,
the river only knows perfection.
Through turbulent drops in elevation,
we pass in panic or elation.
We each choose our disposition,
as our ship of fate changes position.

The River- continued

On this sacred land we walk,
we engage in spirit talk.
We honor spirit in each other,
claiming every other man as
brother.
Every woman as sister, mother.
No family member would we sue.
Love and support is what we do.
This sacred stream
is always flowing.
Water always knows where it is
going.
Flowing always towards the sea.
We too are flowing and shall be
constantly new, recreating
a Divine flow, unabateing.

Seashore Reflections I

I lived alone where salt scents the air.
Oh, how I remember my solitude there,
where an infinite sky and sea both meet,
and giggling waves splash about my feet.

There, seagulls soar in an azure sky.
Time goes unnoticed as days glide by.
Storms come swiftly with wind-lashed rain,
then the sun dissipates the clouds again.

Where the cry of the gulls is a lullaby,
fleecy white clouds scoot across the sky.
There's salty spray in the breeze that blows,
while hot sands sift between my toes.

I return to the shore in memory now,
when concern or worries furrow my brow.
there, all my cares are swept away,
lost in the sea, in its waves and spray.

Seashore Reflections II

I lived alone where the sun bleached my hair.
Oh, how I remember the stickiness there,
where the auto exhaust grays the azure sky,
trash collects as the day goes by.

Winters find the crowd so thick
that suntan lotion forms an oil slick.
Where the cost-of-living soars sky high,
saving accounts glide swiftly by.

There, paper and beer cans and such debris
stretches as far as the eye can see.
Where hot dogs sell for the price of steak,
and students flock at Easter break.

The noise of the crowd drowns the lullaby,
as barroom banners fill the sky.
Where refuse, bottles and cans by the score
make the beaches look like a running sore.

Moonlight Melody

The full moon's light awakened me.
I felt it's ivory glowing.
It called me from my bed to see,
autumn meadow, flowers growing.
Full moon that also calls the sea
to rise high upon the shore
somehow, too, is calling me
to be with her once more.
There's a restlessness within.
I feel, somehow, all undone.
There's a need to begin.
I am a moondrawn one.
Bright moon glow calling me
to come forth and complete
whatever had been left undone.
Where must I place my feet
arising sweetly from my bower.
I spend a pleasant moon lit hour
scribbling moonlit melodies.

Moonsong comes bubbling out of me.
I'm called, with you, to converse,
to share this little moonlit verse.

Fall Break

Fall break, she said, and fall has broken.
Maple leaves on my bacon, a token
of those events of every fall,
from falling nuts to the wild geese call.
The quiet urge for moving south,
apple cider in my mouth.
The smell of autumn leaves a burning
and deep within, a quiet yearning,
to find someone with whom to snuggle
be it witch, wizard, or muggle.
The paintings on glass of Jack Frost,
with stacks of firewood, the cost
of survival through the cold.
Leaves of scarlet, brown and gold.
Leaf lookers abound and the sound of cameras clicking,
the tongue of winters coming, to give us all
a licking.

Autumn

Most of the leaves have fallen.
Those brilliant autumn hues are gone,
all faded now to shades of brown,
soft carpet on our lawn.

Here and there, their smoke's ascending.
That smoky flavor fills the air.
A haze above the distant mountains,
mottled sunshine there.

Apples

This bright fall day
is quite a sight,
oaken fingers reaching right
into puffs of cotton candy.
A day that might prove to be dandy
to cast a line into a stream
or just sit on the bank
and dream.

Autumn dreams in technicolor hues
and perhaps more than a few.
Black walnuts fallen from the tree
which , in time, a cake shall be.
Apples too, for apple pie
And apple butter bye and bye.

Autumn's Days

Somehow a cofferdam
has formed
between my roots and
leaves.

I think that I have energy
but I am deceived.
The freshening flow from
down below
no longer brings the
spark
that lifted me, caused me
to glow.

The light is growing dark.

Night Shadows

Swing Low

Autumn now?
I don't believe it.
Through increasing discomfort,
I perceive the leaves have fallen from the tree.

Aches and pains have come to be,
seemingly without an end.
It's painful just to hold this pen.

Swing low, sweet chariot.

The Struggle

At times I do poorly trying
to paint the world in verse.
Sometimes these brain cells fail me,
and my attempt is worse.

Ah! But on occasion,
the flow of words is sweet,
leaving no abrasion,
and my thoughts are so replete.
With hints of autumn color
that capture life's sweet spirit,
and folks drive for miles,
for the off chance they might hear it.

At times like these, I luxuriate,
like basking in the sun.
I believe that I'll keep writing,
until my days are done.

Fate

Woke up today, so little sleep.
My brain won't engage, and I cannot keep
my focus for more than one minute.
The least force disturbance, and I am in it.

Just lost and wandering afield,
can't ascertain what's false or real,
like walking on a banana peel.
How much longer 'til I heal?

I don't know. I'll have to wait
to determine, now, my fate.

Night Shadows

Black trees loom ominously
against the pale night sky.
Something big and dark in me
sometimes makes me cry.
I weep as one who is bereft
of country, home and friend
and in the darkness contemplate a
hermit's lonely end.

But wait! The night has more than shadows
beneath the slivered moon.
Thousands of tiny lights are winking
their quiet summer tune.
While the crickets all keep cadence,
in the distance cries the loon.

The night's alive with melody
and you can hear it, too.

This poem, my cry, my crickets chirp,
Are calling out to you.

Do you feel the connection?
The threads surround my soul
like some sublimely sweet confection
I long to swallow whole,
to quickly absorb all its essence
and bond, becoming one,
then joined, await together
the coming of the sun.

Fear vs Courage

Like ice cycles dripping down my neck,
icy fingers reaching deep into my soul.
Do I shiver curled in fetal disposition
or assume a new position?

Facing fate and future doubts,
I take the stand that I'm about.

I claim the sun, despite the storm,
bringing in daylight through the darkness,
rising to the dawning of the day,
sparkling, pristine, filled with possibilities.

Lost

Lost, alone, confused, afraid
of each decision that was made
which brought him to this present place,
in which he glimpses, now, his face.

And in those flashes of insight,
the light illuminates what was night.
The night in which his living spark
rushed from each spot in the dark
to just another point unknown,
in which he finds himself alone.

Lost alone, confused, afraid
of each decision that he made.

The Stone

You asked me if I was cold,
and I am not,
yet deep inside a cold wind blows
in a vast vacant spot,
a place where few have ever been,
a very privileged few.

On one hand I could count them all,
though one of them was you.
Holy of holies deep inside
the door now closed is locked.
Because of all that has transpired,
the true heart route is blocked.

Months and years I've slaved and sweat
to roll the stone away.
Today it rolled back itself and
looks like it will stay.

Heavy stone, heavier heart
scarred and withered much apart.

Heavy Heart

In Paradise the leaves have fallen
and we cannot hear birdsong calling.
The joyful sounds of life are missing
and we can hear the serpents hissing.
An arid place now, the grass has withered
the castle is lost in a blizzard
of hate, indifference, and intoxication.
The King has lost his lofty station.
The Prince and Princess are abdicating
to an unknown future that is waiting
but one, for them, they shall create
in a world that isn't filled with hate.
The newest princling that's been born
shall be raised in love and not forelorn
to a castle in decay.
He'll live to see a brighter day
So on this day in which I depart
I do so with a heavy heart.

I'm Here

Grandpa died. I didnt' show.
Hitchhiking home, I was too slow.
My path was guided by the booze.
I could do nothing, then, but lose.

My grandma died and I got drunk.
It really left me in a funk.
When my father died, it broke my heart.
My drinking, too, caused us to part.

The Mother died. I'm still grieving.
Her death, for me, a bitter pill.
Then I lost my little sister.
No words express how much I miss her.

When my stepfather finally passed,
it provided relief, at last.
For one whole year, we watched him die.
There were no more tears left to cry.

With everyone, what now I see,
I was less than I could be.
I was resolved to change my way.
I am here for you today.

A Better Man

The clock begins to sound like thunder,
erasing the illusion I was under,
that somehow, I would live forever.
So, there were many things I never said.
I never did.

And though I regret these great omissions,
it's too late.

Yet, with life's permission,
I'll make what amends I can.
Perhaps, I'll die a better man.

My Father's Shirt

My father's shirt now drapes my chest.
His need for it is gone.
He left his shirt and coat and vest,
his home, his children, and all the rest.
He left his fishing rod and wife
the day that he departed life.

His wardrobe has become my own,
and I go fishing all alone.
I miss the fun we sometimes had,
but most of all, I miss my dad.

The Chasm

Folding back the flowered spread
I lay down on my double bed,
a barren place, a desert waste.
I toss and turn and sleep in haste.

It is an endless broad plateau,
as I lie there it seems to grow.
I fear the vastness of this space
in which I used to see your face.

I'd reach for you and find you there,
and now I grapple empty air.
Sometimes I feel a chasm, black,
where once you lay upon your back,
and if I reach for you I know
I'll fall endlessly to rocks below.
So I cannot sleep at all,
afraid that I may roll and fall.

I seek your presence everywhere,
hungering to stroke your hair,
fingers raking empty air,
multiplied emptiness there.

It's Raining

It's raining. I weep within.
I don't know how I should begin
to tell the tale I have to tell
and in its telling, do it well.

My tears within, a massive tide.
Tidal waves of tears I've cried.
An ebb and flow that floods my soul
with wrenching sobs that leave me cold.

Lost, alone, confused, afraid,
by the decisions I have made,
which carried me to where I stand,
drowning out of sight of land.

I placed my loving hopes in you,
while you, you said you loved me too.
My dreams of happy ever after

awash in tears that drown the laughter.

I knew that we'd be great together,
but here I am in rainy weather.
It's raining out. I weep within,
just don't know how to begin.

The Lonely Darkness

It's after ten and I'm alone
considering the telephone.
It's Sunday night and here I sit,
the nocturnal cafe is dimly lit.
I've not been nocturnal much before,
still, I do not seek the door.

It's after ten and I'm alone
considering the telephone.
This time of night I miss you most,
when all I have of you's a ghost.
The loney dark is filled with voices,
throbbing music fills the air,
I'm painfully aware of all the choices
that brought me here and left you
there.

Wishing you were lying on my
shoulder,

tonight I feel,
somehow much older.

We were connected then, I know.

My transmitter still is sending,
though your receiver doesn't seem to care.
You are on some other channel
and my signals jam the air.
I flip through channels desperately
hoping you'll connect with me.

The loney dark is filled with voices.

The one I listen for is gone,
feeling like I'm out of choices,
sometimes, I feel, I can't go on.

Time

Time, you nasty demon
you really are a thief
you steal all my connections
and leave me only grief.
The clocks ticking sounds,
like thunder,
pronouncing the deadlines we
live under.
All our love lives, deleted,
by the ticking of the clock.
They're all disappearing
tick tock, tick tock, tick tock.
So now's the time for loving,
giving,
today while they're among the living.

The Veil

Standing forth from the veiled earth,
perception, there, is given birth
to notice what's behind the veil.
Is there ought to be bewail?

Once I hid behind a beard,
lest the world see what I feared,
lest the sullied self be seen
and others all that I had been.

The disguises that I wore
oft drew attention to me more.
Those who saw me then were bidden
to discover what was hidden.

It was as though they heard the wail,
"See me here, behind the veil."

Reaper

Gone now, the friends of yesteryears,
evoking yet another tear.

It seems like I am always weeping,
as the reaper comes slowly creeping
around the corner, behind the tree.

He'll be coming soon for me.

Flaming Departure

At eighty five it is surprising
I sit, silently, life revising.
I find my energies shutting down
But notice that I'm still around.
I'm not as finished as I thought
Though, I've been a little overwrought.
Committed to resting on front porch rocking chair.
That's not what living is about
On life's 'front line', find me there
Incapacities of life for me are rife
I don't embrace them and unclaimed
Ignoring them, I live my life
Wide open throttle, going down in flames.

Endgame

The clock's ticking sounds like thunder
declaring the deadline we each live under.
The final moments that we may live,
the last opportunity to give,
to love, to laugh, perhaps to cry.
Gone now, expectations of "Bye Bye."

The bye and byes are no longer there,
gone now our 'anytimes' or 'where's'.

Tick Tock, Tick Tock.

Heart Space

Time and Tide

The ebb and flow of life is sure
and like the sea is never ceasing.

And forever search for me
always leads to the increasing
demands which life cannot fulfill
and leaves us racing, willy-nil
into a future still unknown
until we come into our own.

Perhaps we connect with a seer
whos found a way and shows it to us,
allowing Spirit ever nearer
until, like life, it pulses through us.

Listen for the voice of Spirit.
In the silence you may hear it.

Time stopped

A burst of light as we crossed the crest
to the northern slopes where we saw
the nest
where the Eagles soar
in the azure sky
stopping time as the day goes by.
Yes, time stopped for a moment,
brief.
Time steals our lives,
a quiet thief.
It started again when the
leaves
blew past our windshield
in the autumn breeze.

She Smiles

She smiles and it's like a new moon rising,
full of promise of brightness.

Her eyes shimmer in quiet conversation
which approaches a thunderous roar.
The thunder of that science is like an earthquake
that vibrates the
entire universe to its very core.

She reminds me of every party I never
attended.
I am a constant captive
of those infinitely captivating eyes.

Your Beauty

Your beauty doesn't stop at skin
but everything that lies within.
That skin wrapping makes you whole
because it contains your beautiful soul.
Your soul, your body, and your heart.
Your most magnificent functioning part.
For without that slowing grace
we'd not see the beauty of your face.
The best of beauty is from within
and that shall always take its part.
The control center for the picture
is a warm and loving heart.

Bright Light

Like a lighthouse you radiate,
so filled with light inside.
Like an aurora borealis,
it wells forth as a tide.

Brightness stemming from your smile
and the way that you reach out,
spreading that light of inner joy.
That's what you're about.

Webs

In the soft gray morning light
the webs of sleep lift from the night.
Your body fits mine like a glove,
adhered to me with webs of love.

Sweet faint chords of love's connection,
woven throughout life's perfection.
The rightness of our connected being
makes strong the threads that I am seeing.

I lie here wanting to recapture
the waves we make of divine rapture
when in our joining ecstasy,
I feel you become one with me.

Artist's View

The charcoal and the canvas
are waiting to capture
my impressions of you,
the feelings of rapture.

Skin-the texture of music
on a warm summer's night.
Eyes like dewdrops on roses
in the morning's bright light.

The most difficult task
and the hardest to capture
is the glow from within you
that causes the rapture.

Your lips- the texture of petals of flowers,
I dream of them brushing my own lips for hours.

My vision, like an acid trip, carries me away.
I lust for the canvas and what it may say.

Lost in the Music

I get lost in the music she plays
as she tinkles the ivories and sings,
producing a warmth like a sun's golden rays.
I rejoice in the pleasure it brings.

Notes spill forth like a tinkling stream
in it's burbling trip down the mountain,
like fairy laughter creating a dream
of a moonbeamed rainbowed fountain.

Wrapped in reverie as those notes start to fade,
I trip on the laughter that spills ever after
and swim in the music she's made.

Fire from the Heart

Hearts aflame with burning fire.
The universe be riven
by the heat of love's desire
to be unbound and given.

Precious gems, gold and silver
combined then become art,
increasing value when they're joined
with fire from the heart.

They kindle passion's fire,
consume the drive for gain.
Gifts of love will multiply
and fall as pouring rain.

The Heart of the Story

She was a light unto the darkness.
Her presence was a gift.
For all the world who knew her,
she provided an uplift.

She opened her heart
and opened her doors.
When it came time for giving,
she always gave more.

All we who met her
became a part
of a great loving entity,
as she gave us her heart.

Heaven She Said

I call it Heaven, she said
at the Maples Coffee Shop.
She comes to these mountains
and roves these hills and
never wants to stop.
Wandering forever between green hills
to the songs of whippoorwills,
to the scents of roses in the breeze.
Sometimes it drives me to my knees.
The mountain people we meet
are unusually quiet and sweet.
There's a taste of kindness
in these hills made sweeter by
those whippoorwills.

Waiting

Staring at an empty chair,
envisioning you sitting there.

A window through which sunlight is beaming
and leaves your silver hair a gleaming.

That sweet smile on your face
tells me you have found your place.

Tresses

Her hair; a summer meadow, full
of torrents spinning to her shoulders.
Highlights like ripened fields of wheat
between the mountain boulders.

Their smoothness, a contrast in gray,
lending integrity to the scene.
Sunshine reflecting from her hair,
a warmth that's seldom ever seen.

Ah, what a treasure she possesses
in that warm cataract of tresses.

Heart Space

The sound of love is in a sigh
while tears are forming in the eye,
the colors of violet and blue
within the heart, ring warm and true,
the sounds of waves that break in sighing
while the softness nests in crying.

Golden Years

Time and tide they say
waits for no man.

My experience leads me
to understand
I delight in the fact
that it isn't waiting
So to sustain my place
I paddle, unabating.

Many loves that once were mine
I can no longer see or touch.
But in loving memories
 I embrace them much.
Those now left
keeps me from feeling
so bereft.

My love for you is
always growing.
It warms my heart and
keeps me going.

I look at you and
you are glowing.
In you I see,
sometimes, through tears,
the value of these
golden years.

Goodbye, My love

That's it today,
the only words I've left to say.
Know that I wish for you and yours
the best.
I leave it to God to provide
the rest.

I go to find His place
and peace for me
in some healing spot
beside some sea,
where the salt laden breeze
sings a lullaby
with the pulsing waves
and the seagulls cry.

Where the waves and the sun
can provide a start
for the balm that may heal
A broken heart.

Eternal Ember

Like a dragonfly in amber
I am caught within your
spell.
Seeking to give you
understanding
and to do it oh, so well
that you see the
refractions
of the sun's bright rays
and the glorious
surroundings
I discover as I gaze
there is something so
eternal
in my weak attempt to
grasp
I've seen flashes of glory
that are causing me to
gasp.

Speaking of Love

Sitting at a table in the maples
discussing making love a staple,
how to make it commonplace.

When I sought inclusion
a frown engulfed his face.
Was there some other
product he was trying to create?
Or was it simply that I appeared too
late?

Re-acting as if I was other,
did not we both have
this same Earth as
Mother?

My plea to every listener
is to hold each other nearer.

When you can't be with
the people you love,
just love who you are with.
Discover that you're
Kith and Kin.

Just embrace them, let them in.

Infinity

Infinity's just beyond bare feet,
looking longingly out to sea,
where ocean and sky both meet.
Therein lies eternity.

Beyond long shadows the sun is casting,
beyond the moon shadows cool and still,
there in the distance everlasting,
in the heat of the day or morning's chill.

With ocean breezes in our face,
cries of the gulls in each moment will
aid each in finding that special place.

Where sky and water fuse, we see,
there lies the start of infinity.

Trail Bends

What some see as a fine old ending
is but part of the trail bending.
What some see as darkest night
is where the trail drops out of sight.

Around the bend there is much
that we cannot see or touch.
And just because we cannot see it,
does not mean we shall not be it.

I see her laughing on the trail,
we'll meet again. It cannot fail.
In that much that follows after,
we'll meet again and share our laughter.

Around each bend there is much
that we cannot see or touch.
But because we cannot see it
doesn't mean we shall not be it.

Recovery's Sound

Surcease of sorrow is what I sought.
I seemed, always, to be overwrought.
Sad, depressed, usually aching,
despite the efforts I was making.

Trying hard to change my life,
losing thrice, a lovely wife,
jobs and money, occupations,
seeking for some sweet elation.

I went to meetings when I stopped drinking
and began to work to change my thinking.
Then, one day, I heard this sound,
and there was no one else around.

The sound I heard was my own laughter.
I finally found what I sought after.

The Touch

The touch that I connected to
was filled with power that came through.
As a compounded form of love,
love that fills us from above.
From above, below, within,
in fact there's nowhere to begin.
To describe it's vastness or impact
a surge that has me bouncing back
A recognition of kith and kin
That place where love's seed begins
to overwhelm and overcome
that place which I shall call
Home!

The Colors of Life

What was I pretending not to notice?
What was it I could not see?
Blind spots obscured my vision.
How did I get this warped idea of me?
It may have been in my beginning.
Parental injunction may have played a part.
Creating a game I'm incapable of winning.
Causing my withdrawal from the start.
The start no longer seems to matter.
I've found a way to find the truth.
I no longer resemble some 'Mad Hatter'.
abandoning a path started in my youth
I've discovered a stairway for ascension
 from the dismal swamp I was in.
Now life responds to my intention.
I am no longer what I've been.
I am becoming all I've dreamed of,
better than I thought I could.

To paint a picture of my life today
I'd choose hues from wonderful to good.

Friendship

Last night, the pale, be-misted moon
lit the way for my return,
my return to health and home.
I hadn't gotten here alone.

I've been carried on wings of prayer.
I stumbled, fell, and you were there.
You lifted me and paved the way
to the healthy life I live today.

Pity those who have no friend
on whom they may rely, depend.
My cup is full. It overflows
sufficient for today.
Who knows

if tomorrow's sun shall rise?
I for one must realize,

if it does, you'll be there, too,
to carry me. It's what you do.

So, wherever we may go,
I'll be there for you, you know.

Magic

The reflection each of us adore,
mirrors that living is more.
What we wish for in our living,
manifests, by simply giving.
Everything we wish to see,
is born from deep inside of me.

The Unicorn and the Flower

The unicorn and the flower spoke
in the great meadow neath the oak.
"Tell me, true beautiful lady,
Why don't you grow where it's shady?"

It's so pleasant neath the oak.
Then that lovely lady spoke,
"Oh, great stallion of your race,
I delight to see your face
smiling in the meadow here."

As she spoke, there slid a tear,
from the unicorn's eye to the flower's heart.
"I love you even when we're apart.
I see you in the distant lea
And wish that you were close to me."

Then that lovely lady spoke once more.

"My loving friend that I adore,
I grow only in the warmth of sun,
from which my life force is begun.
I delight when you come by.
I saw that tear fall from your eye.
Look about me and you'll see,
my children that from seed shall be.
My days here shall soon be done,
I shrivel in the late autumn sun."

"Oh! Lovely lady I adore,
you shall be with me evermore.
When your sun filled days are done,
you and I shall become one."

In one gulp he took her in,
that their life together might begin.
Now and forever they are one,
Unicorn and flower neath the sun.

Oxymoron

The blue moon rising silvery bright,
illumined the hills below.
The silver cast upon the grass,
caused them to look like snow.

Com trails crossed beside that moon,
reminding of the current strife,
the *war for peace* we carry on
at an awful cost in life.

We demonize the enemy
and think they're ugly beings,
not noticing how they're so like us,
selecting what we are seeing.

Rebirth

Ah, yes, now I remember
those dark nights of my soul,
with my insides torn asunder.
Would I ever be whole?

Would the sun that shone on others
shine again on me?
From the doom and gloom of my existence
would I once again be free?

I chose to forget myself
and help those who were lost.
In spite of all the pain I felt,
I didn't count the cost.

Now, spring has had its rebirth.
The flowers bloom once more.
though one door has firmly shut,
I've found a different door.

Free

As I gaze around the room
and look upon each face,
through portals of the eyes
to that inner place,

I see a great Pandora's box
behind so many faces.
I see bars and chains and locks
that trap us in our spaces.

And then with just a simple glance,
I see one in the crowd,
dancing a joyful, effervescent dance
that makes me want to shout aloud.

Free! Thank God, at last we're free!

Light at Tunnels End

Now opening shots have been fired.
Quarantine, isolated, and awfully tired
of being unable to see others,
friends, relations, sisters, brothers.
Missing closeness of a friendly face.
At tunnels end there's now a light.
Reintegration's now in sight.

Myself

You're my mirror.
In you, I see myself,
and every one of you
is a tool upon my shelf.

When you share your lives with me,
It's a reflection in which I see
Myself.

Not God

The balance is perfection,
the darkness and the light.
There is nothing but the something
that makes it come out right.

Each and every cell I'm seeing
is part of that eternal being.

Not God! How could that ever be?
Everything that is, is He.

In the beginning, I am.
In the end, I am, too.
When I see my reflection,
I am looking at you.

There is only the oneness,
only the one,
The light of our being
outshines the sun.

The Light

I awoke in the darkness,
but you were there,
lighting my life
like a blazing flare,
living a life that is
filled with the 'Glory'
light that's reflected
from each recovery story.

The stories we share,
each one is a mirror
refracting the light
to each listening hearer.

Every reflection
of the light we share,
a mirror we gaze in
and find ourselves there.

Mirrors

You wrap arms about yourself
as though we were attacking.
You need not create a gulf,
we're all here for your backing.

It may be true that we see you
and all that you are being,
but know this now, we see us, too,
in everything we're seeing.

We're all mirrors, don't you see?
In everything, you're just like me.

Lights, Camera, Action

The lights are on. There's someone home.
We, the living, are not alone.
Together, we are filled with light,
no longer shaken by the night.

Sounds of laughter fill the room,
dispelling even darknest gloom.
Together we have found a way
to turn the darkness into day.

Remembering

I remember why I came.
It is tied, often, to my name.
An infinite being from an
infinite source.

Am I being me? Of course!

I am always in transition,
assuming often a new position.
You may often see my face,
as I assume my newest place.

Living is giving.
Giving is loving.
Loving is God.
God is 'I am'.
We Are.

Oceans.

About the Author

Ocean Shackleton is a United States Veteran, a lover of people with a gift for words. Poet of the Year for 'The Unicorn', Ocean has spent decades writing and composing poetry, drawing from his own experiences of beauty and pain. Currently, he has spent the past few months volunteering to support the effects aiding North Carolina with the aftermath of Hurricane Helene which his forthcoming work will be inspired by.

www.ingramcontent.com/pod-product-compliance
Lightning Source LLC
LaVergne TN
LVHW011211080426
835508LV00007B/730